Cram101 Textbook Outlines to accompany:

Refrigeration and Air Conditioning Technology

Bill Whitman, 6th Edition

A Content Technologies Inc. publication (c) 2012.

Learning System

Cram101 Textbook Outlines is a learning system. The notes in this book are the highlights of your textbook, you will never have to highlight a book again.

How to use this book. Take this book to class, it is your notebook for the lecture. The notes and highlights on the left hand side of the pages follow the outline and order of the textbook. All you have to do is follow along while your instructor presents the lecture. Circle the items emphasized in class and add other important information on the right side. With Cram101 Textbook Outlines you'll spend less time writing and more time listening. Learning becomes more efficient.

Cram101.com Online

Increase your studying efficiency by using Cram101.com's practice tests and online reference material. It is the perfect complement to Cram101 Textbook Outlines. Use self-teaching matching tests or simulate in-class testing with comprehensive multiple choice tests, or simply use Cram's true and false tests for quick review. Cram101.com even allows you to enter your in-class notes for an integrated studying format combining the textbook notes with your class notes.

Visit **www.Cram101.com**, click Sign Up at the top of the screen, and enter **DK73DW11406** in the promo code box on the registration screen. Your access to www.Cram101.com is discounted by 50% because you have purchased this book. Sign up and stop highlighting textbooks forever.

Refrigeration and Air Conditioning Technology
Bill Whitman, 6th

CONTENTS

Chapter 1. Theory of Heat

Metric	In differential geometry, the notion of a metric tensor can be extended to an arbitrary vector bundle. Specifically, if M is a topological manifold and E → M a vector bundle on M, then a metric on E is a bundle map $g : E \times_M E \to M \times R$ from the fiber product of E with itself to the trivial bundle with fiber R such that the restriction of g to each fibre over M is a nondegenerate bilinear map of vector spaces.
Convection	Convection is the movement of molecules within fluids (i.e. liquids, gases) and rheids. It cannot take place in solids, since neither bulk current flows nor significant diffusion can take place in solids. Convection is one of the major modes of heat transfer and mass transfer.
Conditioning	Conditioning on the discrete level Example. A fair coin is tossed 10 times; the random variable X is the number of heads in these 10 tosses, and Y -- the number of heads in the first 3 tosses. In spite of the fact that Y emerges before X it may happen that someone knows X but not Y. Conditional probability Given that X = 1, the conditional probability of the event Y = 0 is P (Y = 0 X = 1) = P (Y = 0, X = 1) / P (X = 1) = 0.7. More generally, $$\mathbb{P}(Y = 0 \mid X = x) = \frac{\binom{7}{x}}{\binom{10}{x}} = \frac{7!(10 - x)!}{(7 - x)!10!}$$

for x = 0, 1, 2, 3, 4, 5, 6, 7; otherwise (for x = 8, 9, 10), P (Y = 0 X = x) = 0. One may also treat the conditional probability as a random variable, -- a function of the random variable X, namely,

$$\mathbb{P}(Y = 0 | X) = \begin{cases} \binom{7}{X} / \binom{10}{X} & \text{for } X \leq 7, \\ 0 & \text{for } X > 7. \end{cases}$$

The expectation of this random variable is equal to the (unconditional) probability,

$$\mathbb{E}(\mathbb{P}(Y = 0 | X)) = \sum_x \mathbb{P}(Y = 0 | X = x) \mathbb{P}(X = x) = \mathbb{P}(Y = 0)$$

namely,

$$\sum_{x=0}^{7} \frac{\binom{7}{x}}{\binom{10}{x}} \cdot \frac{1}{2^{10}} \binom{10}{x} = \frac{1}{8},$$

which is an instance of the law of total probability E (P (A X)) = P (A).

Thus, P (Y = 0 X = 1) may be treated as the value of the random variable P (Y = 0 X) corresponding to X = 1. *On the other hand, P (Y = 0 X = 1) is well-defined irrespective of other possible values of X.*

Conditional expectation

Given that X = 1, the conditional expectation of the random variable Y is E (Y X = 1) = 0.3. More generally,

$$\mathbb{E}(Y | X = x) = \frac{3}{10} x$$

for x = 0, .. 10. (In this example it appears to be a linear function, but in general it is nonlinear).

Chapter 1. Theory of Heat

Efficiency	In statistics, efficiency is a term used in the comparison of various statistical procedures and, in particular, it refers to a measure of the desirability of an estimator, of an experimental design or of an hypothesis testing procedure. The relative efficiency of two procedures is the ratio of their efficiencies, although often this term is used where the comparison is made between a given procedure and a notional "best possible" procedure. The efficiencies and the relative efficiency of two procedures theoretically depend on the sample size available for the given procedure, but it is often possible to use the asymptotic relative efficiency as the principal comparison measure.
Barometer	A barometer is a scientific instrument used to measure atmospheric pressure. It can measure the pressure exerted by the atmosphere by using water, air, or mercury. Pressure tendency can forecast short term changes in the weather.
Density	The mass density is defined as its mass per unit volume. Density is mass divided by volume. The symbol most often used for density is ρ .
Power	The Power of a statistical test is the probability that the test will reject a false null hypothesis (i.e. that it will not make a Type II error). As Power increases, the chances of a Type II error decrease. The probability of a Type II error is referred to as the false negative rate (β). Therefore Power is equal to $1 - \beta$.
Work	In physics, mechanical work is the amount of energy transferred by a force acting through a distance. Like energy, it is a scalar quantity, with SI units of joules. The term work was first coined in 1826 by the French mathematician Gaspard-Gustave Coriolis.
Compression	In functional analysis, the compression of a linear operator T on a Hilbert space to a subspace K is the operator $$P_K T\vert_K$$

Chapter 1. Theory of Heat

where P_K is the orthogonal projection onto K. This is a natural way to obtain an operator on K from an operator on the whole Hilbert space. If K is an invariant subspace for T, then the compression of T to K is the restricted operator K→K sending k to Tk. General, let V be isometry on Hilbert space W, subspace of Hilbert space H (T on H).

Displacement

In fluid mechanics, displacement occurs when an object is immersed in a fluid, pushing it out of the way and taking its place. The volume of the fluid displaced can then be measured, as in the illustration, and from this the volume of the immersed object can be deduced (the volume of the immersed object will be exactly equal to the volume of the displaced fluid).

An object that sinks displaces an amount of fluid equal to the object's volume.

Lead

Lead refers to which set of legs, left or right, leads or advances forward to a greater extent when a quadruped animal is cantering, galloping, or leaping. The feet on the leading side touch the ground forward of its partner. On the "left lead", the animal's left legs lead.

Vibration

Vibration refers to mechanical oscillations about an equilibrium point. The oscillations may be periodic such as the motion of a pendulum or random such as the movement of a tire on a gravel road.

Vibration is occasionally "desirable".

clam101

Chapter 2. Safety, Tools and Equipment, Shop Practices

Connection	In geometry, the notion of a connection makes precise the idea of transporting data along a curve or family of curves in a parallel and consistent manner. There are a variety of kinds of connections in modern geometry, depending on what sort of data one wants to transport. For instance, an affine connection, the most elementary type of connection, gives a means for transporting tangent vectors to a manifold from one point to another along a curve.
Shock	Circulatory shock, commonly known simply as shock, is a serious, life-threatening medical condition defined as an inadequate perfusion of tissues which is insufficient to meet cellular metabolic needs. As the blood carries oxygen and nutrients around the body, reduced flow hinders the delivery of these components to the tissues, and can stop the tissues from functioning properly. The process of blood entering the tissues is called perfusion, so when perfusion is not occurring properly this is called a hypoperfusional (hypo = below) state.
Conditioning	Conditioning on the discrete level

Example. A fair coin is tossed 10 times; the random variable X is the number of heads in these 10 tosses, and Y -- the number of heads in the first 3 tosses. In spite of the fact that Y emerges before X it may happen that someone knows X but not Y.

Conditional probability

Given that X = 1, the conditional probability of the event Y = 0 is
P (Y = 0 X = 1) = P (Y = 0, X = 1) / P (X = 1) = 0.7. More generally,

$$\mathbb{P}(Y=0|X=x) = \frac{\binom{7}{x}}{\binom{10}{x}} = \frac{7!(10-x)!}{(7-x)!10!}$$

for x = 0, 1, 2, 3, 4, 5, 6, 7; otherwise (for x = 8, 9, 10), P (Y = 0 X = x) = 0. One may also treat the conditional probability as a random variable, -- a function of the random variable X, namely,

$$\mathbb{P}(Y=0|X) = \begin{cases} \binom{7}{X}/\binom{10}{X} & \text{for } X \le 7, \\ 0 & \text{for } X > 7. \end{cases}$$

11

The expectation of this random variable is equal to the (unconditional) probability,

$$\mathbb{E}(\mathbb{P}(Y=0|X)) = \sum_x \mathbb{P}(Y=0|X=x)\mathbb{P}(X=x) = \mathbb{P}(Y=0),$$

namely,

$$\sum_{x=0}^{7} \frac{\binom{7}{x}}{\binom{10}{x}} \cdot \frac{1}{2^{10}} \binom{10}{x} = \frac{1}{8},$$

which is an instance of the law of total probability E (P (A X)) = P (A).

Thus, P (Y = 0 X = 1) may be treated as the value of the random variable P (Y = 0 X) corresponding to X = 1. *On the other hand, P (Y = 0 X = 1) is well-defined irrespective of other possible values of X.*

Conditional expectation

Given that X = 1, the conditional expectation of the random variable Y is E (Y X = 1) = 0.3. More generally,

$$\mathbb{E}(Y|X=x) = \frac{3}{10}x$$

for x = 0, .. 10. (In this example it appears to be a linear function, but in general it is nonlinear).

Reduction

In mathematics, reduction refers to the rewriting of an expression into a simpler form. For example, the process of rewriting a fraction into one with the smallest whole-number denominator possible (while keeping the numerator an integer) is called "reducing a fraction". Rewriting a radical (or "root") expression with the smallest possible whole number under the radical symbol is called "reducing a radical".

Clam101

Chapter 2. Safety, Tools and Equipment, Shop Practices

Manifold	In mathematics (specifically in differential geometry and topology) a manifold is a mathematical space that on a small enough scale resembles the Euclidean space of a specific dimension, called the dimension of the manifold. Thus, a line and a circle are one-dimensional manifolds, a plane and sphere (the surface of a ball) are two-dimensional manifolds, and so on into high-dimensional space. More formally, every point of an n-dimensional manifold has a neighborhood homeomorphic to an open subset of the n-dimensional space R^n.
Manifold	In mathematics (specifically in differential geometry and topology) a manifold is a mathematical space that on a small enough scale resembles the Euclidean space of a specific dimension, called the dimension of the manifold. Thus, a line and a circle are one-dimensional manifolds, a plane and sphere (the surface of a ball) are two-dimensional manifolds, and so on into high-dimensional space. More formally, every point of an n-dimensional manifold has a neighborhood homeomorphic to an open subset of the n-dimensional space R^n.
Barometer	A barometer is a scientific instrument used to measure atmospheric pressure. It can measure the pressure exerted by the atmosphere by using water, air, or mercury. Pressure tendency can forecast short term changes in the weather.
Continuous	In probability theory, a probability distribution is called continuous if its cumulative distribution function is continuous. This is equivalent to saying that for random variables X with the distribution in question, $Pr[X = a] = 0$ for all real numbers a, i.e.: the probability that X attains the value a is zero, for any number a. If the distribution of X is continuous then X is called a continuous random variable.
Connector	In mathematics, a connector is a map which can be defined for a linear connection and used to define the covariant derivative on a vector bundle from the linear connection.
Curve	In mathematics, a curve is, generally speaking, an object similar to a line but which is not required to be straight. This entails that a line is a special case of curve, namely a curve with null curvature. Often curves in two-dimensional (plane curves) or three-dimensional (space curves) Euclidean space are of interest.
Efficient	In statistics, an estimator is called efficient if it estimates the parameter of interest in some 'best possible' manner. The notion of 'best possible' relies upon the choice of a particular loss function -- the function which quantifies the relative degree of undesirability of estimation errors of different magnitudes. The most common choice of the loss function is quadratic: $â„"(e) = e^2$, resulting in the mean squared error criterion of optimality.

Chapter 2. Safety, Tools and Equipment, Shop Practices

Lead	Lead refers to which set of legs, left or right, leads or advances forward to a greater extent when a quadruped animal is cantering, galloping, or leaping. The feet on the leading side touch the ground forward of its partner. On the "left lead", the animal's left legs lead.
Solenoid	In mathematics, a solenoid is a compact connected topological space (i.e. a continuum) that may be obtained as the inverse limit of an inverse system of topological groups and continuous homomorphisms $$(S_i, f_i), \quad f_i\colon S_{i+1} \to S_i, \quad i \geq 0,$$ where each S_i is a circle and f_i is the map that uniformly wraps the circle S_{i+1} n_i times ($n_i \geq 2$) around the circle S_i. This construction can be carried out geometrically in the three-dimensional Euclidean space R^3. A solenoid is a one-dimensional homogeneous indecomposable continuum that has the structure of a compact topological group.
Running	Running is a means of terrestrial locomotion allowing a human or an animal to move rapidly on foot. It is simply defined in athletics terms as a gait in which at regular points during the running cycle both feet are off the ground. This is in contrast to walking, where one foot is always in contact with the ground, the legs are kept mostly straight and the center of gravity vaults over the legs in an inverted pendulum fashion.
Control system	A control system is a device or set of devices to manage, command, direct or regulate the behavior of other devices or systems. There are two common classes of control systems, with many variations and combinations: logic or sequential controls, and feedback or linear controls. There is also fuzzy logic, which attempts to combine some of the design simplicity of logic with the utility of linear control.
Regulator	In automatic control, a regulator is a device which has the function of maintaining a designated characteristic. It performs the activity of managing or maintaining a range of values in a machine. The measurable property of a device is managed closely by specified conditions or an advance set value; or it can be a variable according to a predetermined arrangement scheme.

Chapter 2. Safety, Tools and Equipment, Shop Practices

Regulator	In automatic control, a regulator is a device which has the function of maintaining a designated characteristic. It performs the activity of managing or maintaining a range of values in a machine. The measurable property of a device is managed closely by specified conditions or an advance set value; or it can be a variable according to a predetermined arrangement scheme.
Impact	In mechanics, an impact is a high force or shock applied over a short time period when two or more bodies collide. Such a force or acceleration usually has a greater effect than a lower force applied over a proportionally longer time period of time. The effect depends critically on the relative velocity of the bodies to one another.

Chapter 3. Basic Automatic Controls

Electromotive force	In physics, electromotive force, or (occasionally) electromotance is "that which tends to cause current (actual electrons and ions) to flow." More formally, emf is the external work expended per unit of charge to produce an electric potential difference across two open-circuited terminals. The electric potential difference is created by separating positive and negative charges, thereby generating an electric field. The created electrical potential difference drives current flow if a circuit is attached to the source of emf.
Force	In physics, a force is any influence that causes a free body to undergo a change in speed, a change in direction, or a change in shape. Force can also be described by intuitive concepts such as a push or pull that can cause an object with mass to change its velocity (which includes to begin moving from a state of rest), i.e., to accelerate, or which can cause a flexible object to deform. A force has both magnitude and direction, making it a vector quantity.
Contact	In mathematics, contact of order k of functions is an equivalence relation, corresponding to having the same value at a point P and also the same derivatives there, up to order k. The equivalence classes are generally called jets. The point of osculation is also called the double cusp.
Series	A series is the sum of the terms of a sequence. Finite sequences and series have defined first and last terms, whereas infinite sequences and series continue indefinitely. In mathematics, given an infinite sequence of numbers $\{ a_n \}$, a series is informally the result of adding all those terms together: $a_1 + a_2 + a_3 + \cdots$.
Power	The Power of a statistical test is the probability that the test will reject a false null hypothesis (i.e. that it will not make a Type II error). As Power increases, the chances of a Type II error decrease. The probability of a Type II error is referred to as the false negative rate (β). Therefore Power is equal to $1 - \beta$.

Chapter 3. Basic Automatic Controls

Inductance	Inductance is the property of an electrical circuit causing voltage to be generated proportional to the rate of change in current in a circuit. This property also is called self inductance to discriminate it from mutual inductance, describing the voltage induced in one electrical circuit by the rate of change of the electric current in another circuit.
	The quantitative definition of the self inductance L of an electrical circuit in SI units (webers per ampere, known as henries) is $$v = L\frac{di}{dt},$$ where v denotes the voltage in volts and i the current in amperes.
Eddy current	Eddy currents (also called Foucault currents) are currents induced in conductors, opposing the change in flux that generated them. It is caused when a conductor is exposed to a changing magnetic field due to relative motion of the field source and conductor; or due to variations of the field with time. This can cause a circulating flow of electrons, or a current, within the body of the conductor.
Current	In mathematics, more particularly in functional analysis, differential topology, and geometric measure theory, a k-current in the sense of Georges de Rham is a functional on the space of compactly supported differential k-forms, on a smooth manifold M. Formally currents behave like Schwartz distributions on a space of differential forms. In a geometric setting, they can represent integration over a submanifold, generalizing the Dirac delta function, or more generally even directional derivatives of delta functions (multipoles) spread out along subsets of M.
	Let $\Omega_c^m\left(\mathbb{R}^n\right)$ denote the space of smooth m-forms with compact support on R^n. A current is a linear functional on $\Omega_c^m\left(\mathbb{R}^n\right)$ which is continuous in the sense of distributions.

Chapter 3. Basic Automatic Controls

Fault	In geology, a fault is a planar fracture or discontinuity in a volume of rock, across which there has been significant displacement. Large faults within the Earth's crust result from the action of tectonic forces. Energy release associated with rapid movement on active faults is the cause of most earthquakes, such as occurs on the San Andreas Fault, California.
Fluid	In physics, a fluid is a substance that continually deforms (flows) under an applied shear stress, no matter how small. Fluids are a subset of the phases of matter and include liquids, gases, plasmas and, to some extent, plastic solids.
	In common usage, "fluid" is often used as a synonym for "liquid", with no implication that gas could also be present.
Diaphragm	In mechanics, a diaphragm is a sheet of a semi-flexible material anchored at its periphery and most often round in shape. It serves either as a barrier between two chambers, moving slightly up into one chamber or down into the other depending on differences in pressure, or as a device that vibrates when certain frequencies are applied to it.
	A diaphragm pump uses a diaphragm to pump a fluid.
Action	In physics, action is an attribute of the dynamics of a physical system. It is a mathematical functional which takes the trajectory, also called path or history, of the system as its argument and has a real number as its result. Action has the dimension of energy × time, and its unit is joule-seconds in the International System of Units (SI).
Swing	An electoral swing analysis (or swing) shows the extent of change in voter support from one election to another. It is an indicator of voter support for individual candidates or political parties, or voter preference between two or more candidates or parties. A swing can be calculated for the electorate as a whole, or for a given electoral district or demographic.
Mechanism	Mechanism is the belief that natural wholes (principally living things) are like machines or artifacts, composed of parts lacking any intrinsic relationship to each other, and with their order imposed from without. Thus, the source of an apparent thing's activities is not the whole itself, but its parts or an external influence on the parts. Mechanism is opposed to the organic conception of nature best articulated by Aristotle and more recently elaborated as vitalism.

Chapter 3. Basic Automatic Controls

Fluid	In physics, a fluid is a substance that continually deforms (flows) under an applied shear stress, no matter how small. Fluids are a subset of the phases of matter and include liquids, gases, plasmas and, to some extent, plastic solids.
	In common usage, "fluid" is often used as a synonym for "liquid", with no implication that gas could also be present.
Flow	In mathematics, a flow or superfunction generalizes n-fold iteration of functions so that the iteration count n becomes a continuous parameter. It is used to formalize in mathematical terms the general idea of "a variable that depends on time" that occurs very frequently in engineering, physics and the study of ordinary differential equations. Informally, if x(t) is some coordinate of some system that behaves continuously as a function of t, then x(t) is a flow.
Solenoid	In mathematics, a solenoid is a compact connected topological space (i.e. a continuum) that may be obtained as the inverse limit of an inverse system of topological groups and continuous homomorphisms $$(S_i, f_i), \quad f_i: S_{i+1} \to S_i, \quad i \geq 0,$$ where each S_i is a circle and f_i is the map that uniformly wraps the circle S_{i+1} n_i times ($n_i \geq 2$) around the circle S_i. This construction can be carried out geometrically in the three-dimensional Euclidean space R^3. A solenoid is a one-dimensional homogeneous indecomposable continuum that has the structure of a compact topological group.
Differential	In calculus, a differential is traditionally an infinitesimally small change in a variable. For example, if x is a variable, then a change in the value of x is often denoted Δx (or δx when this change is considered to be small). The differential dx represents such a change, but is infinitely small.
Regulator	In automatic control, a regulator is a device which has the function of maintaining a designated characteristic. It performs the activity of managing or maintaining a range of values in a machine. The measurable property of a device is managed closely by specified conditions or an advance set value; or it can be a variable according to a predetermined arrangement scheme.

Chapter 3. Basic Automatic Controls

Nozzle	A nozzle is a mechanical device designed to control the direction or characteristics of a fluid flow as it exits (or enters) an enclosed chamber or pipe via an orifice.
	A nozzle is often a pipe or tube of varying cross sectional area, and it can be used to direct or modify the flow of a fluid (liquid or gas). Nozzles are frequently used to control the rate of flow, speed, direction, mass, shape, and/or the pressure of the stream that emerges from them.
Control system	A control system is a device or set of devices to manage, command, direct or regulate the behavior of other devices or systems.
	There are two common classes of control systems, with many variations and combinations: logic or sequential controls, and feedback or linear controls. There is also fuzzy logic, which attempts to combine some of the design simplicity of logic with the utility of linear control.

Chapter 4. Electric Motors

Slip	In vehicle dynamics, slip is the relative motion between a tire and the road surface it is moving on. This slip can be generated either by the tire's rotational speed being greater or less than the free-rolling speed (usually described as percent slip), or by the tire's plane of rotation being at an angle to its direction of motion (referred to as slip angle). The slip is generally given as a percentage of the difference between the surface speed of the wheel compared to the speed between axis and road surface, as: $$slip = \frac{\omega r - v}{v},$$ where ω is rotational speed of the wheel, r is wheel radius and v is vehicle speed.
Running	Running is a means of terrestrial locomotion allowing a human or an animal to move rapidly on foot. It is simply defined in athletics terms as a gait in which at regular points during the running cycle both feet are off the ground. This is in contrast to walking, where one foot is always in contact with the ground, the legs are kept mostly straight and the center of gravity vaults over the legs in an inverted pendulum fashion.
Power	The Power of a statistical test is the probability that the test will reject a false null hypothesis (i.e. that it will not make a Type II error). As Power increases, the chances of a Type II error decrease. The probability of a Type II error is referred to as the false negative rate (β). Therefore Power is equal to $1 - β$.
Electromotive force	In physics, electromotive force, or (occasionally) electromotance is "that which tends to cause current (actual electrons and ions) to flow." More formally, emf is the external work expended per unit of charge to produce an electric potential difference across two open-circuited terminals. The electric potential difference is created by separating positive and negative charges, thereby generating an electric field. The created electrical potential difference drives current flow if a circuit is attached to the source of emf.

Chapter 4. Electric Motors

Force

In physics, a force is any influence that causes a free body to undergo a change in speed, a change in direction, or a change in shape. Force can also be described by intuitive concepts such as a push or pull that can cause an object with mass to change its velocity (which includes to begin moving from a state of rest), i.e., to accelerate, or which can cause a flexible object to deform. A force has both magnitude and direction, making it a vector quantity.

Current

In mathematics, more particularly in functional analysis, differential topology, and geometric measure theory, a k-current in the sense of Georges de Rham is a functional on the space of compactly supported differential k-forms, on a smooth manifold M. Formally currents behave like Schwartz distributions on a space of differential forms. In a geometric setting, they can represent integration over a submanifold, generalizing the Dirac delta function, or more generally even directional derivatives of delta functions (multipoles) spread out along subsets of M.

Let $\Omega_c^m\left(\mathbb{R}^n\right)$ denote the space of smooth m-forms with compact support on R^n. A current is a linear functional on $\Omega_c^m\left(\mathbb{R}^n\right)$ which is continuous in the sense of distributions.

Frequency

Frequency is the number of occurrences of a repeating event per unit time. It is also referred to as temporal frequency. The period is the duration of one cycle in a repeating event, so the period is the reciprocal of the frequency.

Connector

In mathematics, a connector is a map which can be defined for a linear connection and used to define the covariant derivative on a vector bundle from the linear connection.

Regulator

In automatic control, a regulator is a device which has the function of maintaining a designated characteristic. It performs the activity of managing or maintaining a range of values in a machine. The measurable property of a device is managed closely by specified conditions or an advance set value; or it can be a variable according to a predetermined arrangement scheme.

Chapter 4. Electric Motors

Compression	In functional analysis, the compression of a linear operator T on a Hilbert space to a subspace K is the operator $$P_K T\|_K$$ where P_K is the orthogonal projection onto K. This is a natural way to obtain an operator on K from an operator on the whole Hilbert space. If K is an invariant subspace for T, then the compression of T to K is the restricted operator K→K sending k to Tk. General, let V be isometry on Hilbert space W, subspace of Hilbert space H (T on H).
Manifold	In mathematics (specifically in differential geometry and topology) a manifold is a mathematical space that on a small enough scale resembles the Euclidean space of a specific dimension, called the dimension of the manifold. Thus, a line and a circle are one-dimensional manifolds, a plane and sphere (the surface of a ball) are two-dimensional manifolds, and so on into high-dimensional space. More formally, every point of an n-dimensional manifold has a neighborhood homeomorphic to an open subset of the n-dimensional space R^n.
Diaphragm	In mechanics, a diaphragm is a sheet of a semi-flexible material anchored at its periphery and most often round in shape. It serves either as a barrier between two chambers, moving slightly up into one chamber or down into the other depending on differences in pressure, or as a device that vibrates when certain frequencies are applied to it. A diaphragm pump uses a diaphragm to pump a fluid.
Resistance	"Resistance" as initially used by Sigmund Freud, referred to patients blocking memories from conscious memory. This was a key concept, since the primary treatment method of Freud's talk therapy required making these memories available to the patient's consciousness. "Resistance" expanded

Chapter 4. Electric Motors

Later, Freud described five different forms of resistance.

Pulley

A pulley, is a mechanism composed of a wheel on an axle or shaft that may have a groove between two flanges around its circumference. A rope, cable, belt, or chain usually runs over the wheel and inside the groove, if present. Pulleys are used to change the direction of an applied force, transmit rotational motion, or realize a mechanical advantage in either a linear or rotational system of motion.

Conditioning	Conditioning on the discrete level

Example. A fair coin is tossed 10 times; the random variable X is the number of heads in these 10 tosses, and Y -- the number of heads in the first 3 tosses. In spite of the fact that Y emerges before X it may happen that someone knows X but not Y.

Conditional probability

Given that X = 1, the conditional probability of the event Y = 0 is
P (Y = 0 X = 1) = P (Y = 0, X = 1) / P (X = 1) = 0.7. More generally,

$$\mathbb{P}(Y = 0 | X = x) = \frac{\binom{7}{x}}{\binom{10}{x}} = \frac{7!(10 - x)!}{(7 - x)!10!}$$

for x = 0, 1, 2, 3, 4, 5, 6, 7; otherwise (for x = 8, 9, 10), P (Y = 0 X = x) = 0. One may also treat the conditional probability as a random variable, -- a function of the random variable X, namely,

$$\mathbb{P}(Y = 0 | X) = \begin{cases} \binom{7}{X} / \binom{10}{X} & \text{for } X \leq 7, \\ 0 & \text{for } X > 7. \end{cases}$$

The expectation of this random variable is equal to the (unconditional) probability,

$$\mathbb{E}(\mathbb{P}(Y = 0 | X)) = \sum_x \mathbb{P}(Y = 0 | X = x)\mathbb{P}(X = x) = \mathbb{P}(Y = 0),$$

namely,

$$\sum_{x=0}^{7} \frac{\binom{7}{x}}{\binom{10}{x}} \cdot \frac{1}{2^{10}} \binom{10}{x} = \frac{1}{8},$$

which is an instance of the law of total probability E (P (A X)) = P (A).

Thus, P (Y = 0 X = 1) may be treated as the value of the random variable P (Y = 0 X) corresponding to X = 1. *On the other hand, P (Y = 0 X = 1) is well-defined irrespective of other possible values of X.*

Conditional expectation

Given that X = 1, the conditional expectation of the random variable Y is E (Y X = 1) = 0.3. More generally,

$$\mathbb{E}(Y|X = x) = \frac{3}{10}x$$

for x = 0, .. 10. (In this example it appears to be a linear function, but in general it is nonlinear).

Efficiency

In statistics, efficiency is a term used in the comparison of various statistical procedures and, in particular, it refers to a measure of the desirability of an estimator, of an experimental design or of an hypothesis testing procedure.

The relative efficiency of two procedures is the ratio of their efficiencies, although often this term is used where the comparison is made between a given procedure and a notional "best possible" procedure. The efficiencies and the relative efficiency of two procedures theoretically depend on the sample size available for the given procedure, but it is often possible to use the asymptotic relative efficiency as the principal comparison measure.

Chapter 5. Commercial Refrigeration

Current

In mathematics, more particularly in functional analysis, differential topology, and geometric measure theory, a k-current in the sense of Georges de Rham is a functional on the space of compactly supported differential k-forms, on a smooth manifold M. Formally currents behave like Schwartz distributions on a space of differential forms. In a geometric setting, they can represent integration over a submanifold, generalizing the Dirac delta function, or more generally even directional derivatives of delta functions (multipoles) spread out along subsets of M.

Let $\Omega_c^m(\mathbb{R}^n)$ denote the space of smooth m-forms with compact support on R^n. A current is a linear functional on $\Omega_c^m(\mathbb{R}^n)$ which is continuous in the sense of distributions.

Specification

In regression analysis and related fields such as econometrics, specification is the process of converting a theory into a regression model. This process consists of selecting an appropriate functional form for the model and choosing which variables to include. Model specification is one of the first steps in regression analysis.

Compression

In functional analysis, the compression of a linear operator T on a Hilbert space to a subspace K is the operator

$$P_K T|_K$$

where P_K is the orthogonal projection onto K. This is a natural way to obtain an operator on K from an operator on the whole Hilbert space. If K is an invariant subspace for T, then the compression of T to K is the restricted operator K→K sending k to Tk. General, let V be isometry on Hilbert space W, subspace of Hilbert space H (T on H).

Filtration

In mathematics, a filtration is an indexed set S_i of subobjects of a given algebraic structure S, with the index i running over some index set I that is a totally ordered set, subject to the condition that if i ≤ j in I then $S_i \subseteq S_j$. The concept dual to a filtration is called a cofiltration.

Sometimes, as in a filtered algebra, there is instead the requirement that the S_i be subobjects with respect to certain operations (say, vector addition), but with respect to other operations (say, multiplication), they instead satisfy $S_i \cdot S_j \subset S_{i+j}$, where here the index set is the natural numbers; this is by analogy with a graded algebra.

Differential	In calculus, a differential is traditionally an infinitesimally small change in a variable. For example, if x is a variable, then a change in the value of x is often denoted Δx (or δx when this change is considered to be small). The differential dx represents such a change, but is infinitely small.
Manifold	In mathematics (specifically in differential geometry and topology) a manifold is a mathematical space that on a small enough scale resembles the Euclidean space of a specific dimension, called the dimension of the manifold. Thus, a line and a circle are one-dimensional manifolds, a plane and sphere (the surface of a ball) are two-dimensional manifolds, and so on into high-dimensional space. More formally, every point of an n-dimensional manifold has a neighborhood homeomorphic to an open subset of the n-dimensional space R^n.
Running	Running is a means of terrestrial locomotion allowing a human or an animal to move rapidly on foot. It is simply defined in athletics terms as a gait in which at regular points during the running cycle both feet are off the ground. This is in contrast to walking, where one foot is always in contact with the ground, the legs are kept mostly straight and the center of gravity vaults over the legs in an inverted pendulum fashion.
Mechanism	Mechanism is the belief that natural wholes (principally living things) are like machines or artifacts, composed of parts lacking any intrinsic relationship to each other, and with their order imposed from without. Thus, the source of an apparent thing's activities is not the whole itself, but its parts or an external influence on the parts. Mechanism is opposed to the organic conception of nature best articulated by Aristotle and more recently elaborated as vitalism.
Involute	In the differential geometry of curves, an involute is a curve obtained from another given curve by attaching an imaginary taut string to the given curve and tracing its free end as it is wound onto that given curve; or in reverse, unwound. It is a roulette wherein the rolling curve is a straight line containing the generating point. For example, an involute approximates the path followed by a tetherball as the connecting tether is wound around the center pole.

Chapter 5. Commercial Refrigeration

Control system	A control system is a device or set of devices to manage, command, direct or regulate the behavior of other devices or systems. There are two common classes of control systems, with many variations and combinations: logic or sequential controls, and feedback or linear controls. There is also fuzzy logic, which attempts to combine some of the design simplicity of logic with the utility of linear control.
Diaphragm	In mechanics, a diaphragm is a sheet of a semi-flexible material anchored at its periphery and most often round in shape. It serves either as a barrier between two chambers, moving slightly up into one chamber or down into the other depending on differences in pressure, or as a device that vibrates when certain frequencies are applied to it. A diaphragm pump uses a diaphragm to pump a fluid.
Transmission	A transmission or gearbox provides speed and torque conversions from a rotating power source to another device using gear ratios. In British English the term transmission refers to the whole drive train, including gearbox, clutch, prop shaft (for rear-wheel drive), differential and final drive shafts. In American English, however, the distinction is made that a gearbox is any device which converts speed and torque, whereas a transmission is a type of gearbox that can be "shifted" to dynamically change the speed:torque ratio, such as in a vehicle.
Solenoid	In mathematics, a solenoid is a compact connected topological space (i.e. a continuum) that may be obtained as the inverse limit of an inverse system of topological groups and continuous homomorphisms $$(S_i, f_i), \quad f_i: S_{i+1} \rightarrow S_i, \quad i \geq 0,$$ where each S_i is a circle and f_i is the map that uniformly wraps the circle S_{i+1} n_i times ($n_i \geq 2$) around the circle S_i. This construction can be carried out geometrically in the three-dimensional Euclidean space R^3. A solenoid is a one-dimensional homogeneous indecomposable continuum that has the structure of a compact topological group.

Chapter 5. Commercial Refrigeration

PID controller	A proportional-integral-derivative controller (PID controller) is a generic control loop feedback mechanism (controller) widely used in industrial control systems - a PID is the most commonly used feedback controller. A PID controller calculates an "error" value as the difference between a measured process variable and a desired setpoint. The controller attempts to minimize the error by adjusting the process control inputs.
Derivative	In calculus, a branch of mathematics, the derivative is a measure of how a function changes as its input changes. Loosely speaking, a derivative can be thought of as how much one quantity is changing in response to changes in some other quantity; for example, the derivative of the position of a moving object with respect to time is the object's instantaneous velocity. Conversely, the integral of the object's velocity over time is how much the object's position changes from the time when the integral begins to the time when the integral ends.
Integral	Integration is an important concept in mathematics and, together with differentiation, is one of the two main operations in calculus. Given a function f of a real variable x and an interval [a, b] of the real line, the definite integral $$\int_a^b f(x)\,dx$$ is defined informally to be the net signed area of the region in the xy-plane bounded by the graph of f, the x-axis, and the vertical lines x = a and x = b. The term integral may also refer to the notion of antiderivative, a function F whose derivative is the given function f.
Curve	In mathematics, a curve is, generally speaking, an object similar to a line but which is not required to be straight. This entails that a line is a special case of curve, namely a curve with null curvature. Often curves in two-dimensional (plane curves) or three-dimensional (space curves) Euclidean space are of interest.
Regulator	In automatic control, a regulator is a device which has the function of maintaining a designated characteristic. It performs the activity of managing or maintaining a range of values in a machine. The measurable property of a device is managed closely by specified conditions or an advance set value; or it can be a variable according to a predetermined arrangement scheme.

Chapter 5. Commercial Refrigeration

Current

In mathematics, more particularly in functional analysis, differential topology, and geometric measure theory, a k-current in the sense of Georges de Rham is a functional on the space of compactly supported differential k-forms, on a smooth manifold M. Formally currents behave like Schwartz distributions on a space of differential forms. In a geometric setting, they can represent integration over a submanifold, generalizing the Dirac delta function, or more generally even directional derivatives of delta functions (multipoles) spread out along subsets of M.

Let $\Omega_c^m(\mathbb{R}^n)$ denote the space of smooth m-forms with compact support on $\mathbb{R}^n$. A current is a linear functional on $\Omega_c^m(\mathbb{R}^n)$ which is continuous in the sense of distributions.

Nozzle

A nozzle is a mechanical device designed to control the direction or characteristics of a fluid flow as it exits (or enters) an enclosed chamber or pipe via an orifice.

A nozzle is often a pipe or tube of varying cross sectional area, and it can be used to direct or modify the flow of a fluid (liquid or gas). Nozzles are frequently used to control the rate of flow, speed, direction, mass, shape, and/or the pressure of the stream that emerges from them.

Mixing

In mathematics, mixing is an abstract concept originating from physics: the attempt to describe the irreversible thermodynamic process of mixing in the everyday world: mixing paint, mixing drinks, etc.

The concept appears in ergodic theory--the study of stochastic processes and measure-preserving dynamical systems. Several different definitions for mixing exist, including strong mixing, weak mixing and topological mixing, with the last not requiring a measure to be defined.

51

Chapter 5. Commercial Refrigeration

Core	In anatomy, the core refers, in its most general of definitions, to the body minus the legs and arms. Functional movements are highly dependent on the core, and lack of core development can result in a predisposition to injury. The major muscles of the core reside in the area of the belly and the mid and lower back (not the shoulders), and peripherally include the hips, the shoulders and the neck.
Connection	In geometry, the notion of a connection makes precise the idea of transporting data along a curve or family of curves in a parallel and consistent manner. There are a variety of kinds of connections in modern geometry, depending on what sort of data one wants to transport. For instance, an affine connection, the most elementary type of connection, gives a means for transporting tangent vectors to a manifold from one point to another along a curve.
Vibration	Vibration refers to mechanical oscillations about an equilibrium point. The oscillations may be periodic such as the motion of a pendulum or random such as the movement of a tire on a gravel road. Vibration is occasionally "desirable".
Force	In physics, a force is any influence that causes a free body to undergo a change in speed, a change in direction, or a change in shape. Force can also be described by intuitive concepts such as a push or pull that can cause an object with mass to change its velocity (which includes to begin moving from a state of rest), i.e., to accelerate, or which can cause a flexible object to deform. A force has both magnitude and direction, making it a vector quantity.
Matching	The matching is a statistical technique which is used to evaluate the effect of a treatment by comparing the treated and the non-treated in non experimental design (when the treatment is not randomly assigned). People use this technique with observational data (ie non experimental data). The idea is to find for any treated unit a similar non treated unit with similar observable characteristics.
Fluid	In physics, a fluid is a substance that continually deforms (flows) under an applied shear stress, no matter how small. Fluids are a subset of the phases of matter and include liquids, gases, plasmas and, to some extent, plastic solids.

	In common usage, "fluid" is often used as a synonym for "liquid", with no implication that gas could also be present.
Impact	In mechanics, an impact is a high force or shock applied over a short time period when two or more bodies collide. Such a force or acceleration usually has a greater effect than a lower force applied over a proportionally longer time period of time. The effect depends critically on the relative velocity of the bodies to one another.
Connector	In mathematics, a connector is a map which can be defined for a linear connection and used to define the covariant derivative on a vector bundle from the linear connection.
Foundation	A foundation is a structure that transfers loads to the earth. Foundations are generally broken into two categories: shallow foundations and deep foundations. Footing types Shallow footings Shallow footings are, usually, embedded a meter or so into soil.
Distribution	In differential geometry, a discipline within mathematics, a distribution is a subset of the tangent bundle of a manifold satisfying certain properties.
Cube	In geometry, a cube is a three-dimensional solid object bounded by six square faces, facets or sides, with three meeting at each vertex. The cube can also be called a regular hexahedron and is one of the five Platonic solids. It is a special kind of square prism, of rectangular parallelepiped and of trigonal trapezohedron.
Event	In probability theory, an event is a set of outcomes (a subset of the sample space) to which a probability is assigned. Typically, when the sample space is finite, any subset of the sample space is an event. However, this approach does not work well in cases where the sample space is infinite, most notably when the outcome is a real number.

Chapter 6. Air Conditioning (Heating and Humidification)

Resistance	"Resistance" as initially used by Sigmund Freud, referred to patients blocking memories from conscious memory. This was a key concept, since the primary treatment method of Freud's talk therapy required making these memories available to the patient's consciousness. "Resistance" expanded Later, Freud described five different forms of resistance.
Manifold	In mathematics (specifically in differential geometry and topology) a manifold is a mathematical space that on a small enough scale resembles the Euclidean space of a specific dimension, called the dimension of the manifold. Thus, a line and a circle are one-dimensional manifolds, a plane and sphere (the surface of a ball) are two-dimensional manifolds, and so on into high-dimensional space. More formally, every point of an n-dimensional manifold has a neighborhood homeomorphic to an open subset of the n-dimensional space R^n.
Column	A column in structural engineering is a vertical structural element that transmits, through compression, the weight of the structure above to other structural elements below. For the purpose of wind or earthquake engineering, columns may be designed to resist lateral forces. Other compression members are often termed "columns" because of the similar stress conditions.
Manifold	In mathematics (specifically in differential geometry and topology) a manifold is a mathematical space that on a small enough scale resembles the Euclidean space of a specific dimension, called the dimension of the manifold. Thus, a line and a circle are one-dimensional manifolds, a plane and sphere (the surface of a ball) are two-dimensional manifolds, and so on into high-dimensional space. More formally, every point of an n-dimensional manifold has a neighborhood homeomorphic to an open subset of the n-dimensional space R^n.
Regulator	In automatic control, a regulator is a device which has the function of maintaining a designated characteristic. It performs the activity of managing or maintaining a range of values in a machine. The measurable property of a device is managed closely by specified conditions or an advance set value; or it can be a variable according to a predetermined arrangement scheme.

Chapter 6. Air Conditioning (Heating and Humidification)

Diaphragm	In mechanics, a diaphragm is a sheet of a semi-flexible material anchored at its periphery and most often round in shape. It serves either as a barrier between two chambers, moving slightly up into one chamber or down into the other depending on differences in pressure, or as a device that vibrates when certain frequencies are applied to it.
	A diaphragm pump uses a diaphragm to pump a fluid.
Solenoid	In mathematics, a solenoid is a compact connected topological space (i.e. a continuum) that may be obtained as the inverse limit of an inverse system of topological groups and continuous homomorphisms
	$$(S_i, f_i), \quad f_i: S_{i+1} \to S_i, \quad i \geq 0,$$
	where each S_i is a circle and f_i is the map that uniformly wraps the circle S_{i+1} n_i times ($n_i \geq 2$) around the circle S_i. This construction can be carried out geometrically in the three-dimensional Euclidean space R^3. A solenoid is a one-dimensional homogeneous indecomposable continuum that has the structure of a compact topological group.
Primary	A primary is the main physical body of a gravitationally-bound, multi-object system. This body contributes most of the mass of that system and will generally be located near its center of mass.
	In the solar system, the Sun is the primary for all objects that orbit around it.

Chapter 6. Air Conditioning (Heating and Humidification)

Current	In mathematics, more particularly in functional analysis, differential topology, and geometric measure theory, a k-current in the sense of Georges de Rham is a functional on the space of compactly supported differential k-forms, on a smooth manifold M. Formally currents behave like Schwartz distributions on a space of differential forms. In a geometric setting, they can represent integration over a submanifold, generalizing the Dirac delta function, or more generally even directional derivatives of delta functions (multipoles) spread out along subsets of M. Let $\Omega_c^m(\mathbb{R}^n)$ denote the space of smooth m-forms with compact support on R^n. A current is a linear functional on $\Omega_c^m(\mathbb{R}^n)$ which is continuous in the sense of distributions.
Continuous	In probability theory, a probability distribution is called continuous if its cumulative distribution function is continuous. This is equivalent to saying that for random variables X with the distribution in question, Pr[X = a] = 0 for all real numbers a, i.e.: the probability that X attains the value a is zero, for any number a. If the distribution of X is continuous then X is called a continuous random variable.
Compression	In functional analysis, the compression of a linear operator T on a Hilbert space to a subspace K is the operator $$P_K T\|_K$$ where P_K is the orthogonal projection onto K. This is a natural way to obtain an operator on K from an operator on the whole Hilbert space. If K is an invariant subspace for T, then the compression of T to K is the restricted operator K→K sending k to Tk. General, let V be isometry on Hilbert space W, subspace of Hilbert space H (T on H).
Connection	In geometry, the notion of a connection makes precise the idea of transporting data along a curve or family of curves in a parallel and consistent manner. There are a variety of kinds of connections in modern geometry, depending on what sort of data one wants to transport. For instance, an affine connection, the most elementary type of connection, gives a means for transporting tangent vectors to a manifold from one point to another along a curve.

Chapter 6. Air Conditioning (Heating and Humidification)

Efficiency	In statistics, efficiency is a term used in the comparison of various statistical procedures and, in particular, it refers to a measure of the desirability of an estimator, of an experimental design or of an hypothesis testing procedure.

The relative efficiency of two procedures is the ratio of their efficiencies, although often this term is used where the comparison is made between a given procedure and a notional "best possible" procedure. The efficiencies and the relative efficiency of two procedures theoretically depend on the sample size available for the given procedure, but it is often possible to use the asymptotic relative efficiency as the principal comparison measure. |
| Viscosity | Viscosity is a measure of the resistance of a fluid which is being deformed by either shear stress or tensile stress. In everyday terms (and for fluids only), viscosity is "thickness" or "internal friction". Thus, water is "thin", having a lower viscosity, while honey is "thick", having a higher viscosity. |
| Filtration | In mathematics, a filtration is an indexed set S_i of subobjects of a given algebraic structure S, with the index i running over some index set I that is a totally ordered set, subject to the condition that if i ≤ j in I then $S_i \subseteq S_j$. The concept dual to a filtration is called a cofiltration.

Sometimes, as in a filtered algebra, there is instead the requirement that the S_i be subobjects with respect to certain operations (say, vector addition), but with respect to other operations (say, multiplication), they instead satisfy $S_i \cdot S_j \subset S_{i+j}$, where here the index set is the natural numbers; this is by analogy with a graded algebra. |
| Residue | In mathematics, more specifically complex analysis, the residue is a complex number equal to the contour integral of a meromorphic function along a path enclosing one of its singularities. Residues can be computed quite easily and, once known, allow the determination of general contour integrals via the residue theorem. |

The residue of a meromorphic function f at an isolated singularity a, often denoted $\mathrm{Res}(f, a)$ is the unique value R such that f(z) − R / (z − a) has an analytic antiderivative in a punctured disk $0 < |z - a| < \delta$.

Contact

In mathematics, contact of order k of functions is an equivalence relation, corresponding to having the same value at a point P and also the same derivatives there, up to order k. The equivalence classes are generally called jets. The point of osculation is also called the double cusp.

Nozzle

A nozzle is a mechanical device designed to control the direction or characteristics of a fluid flow as it exits (or enters) an enclosed chamber or pipe via an orifice.

A nozzle is often a pipe or tube of varying cross sectional area, and it can be used to direct or modify the flow of a fluid (liquid or gas). Nozzles are frequently used to control the rate of flow, speed, direction, mass, shape, and/or the pressure of the stream that emerges from them.

Nozzle

A nozzle is a mechanical device designed to control the direction or characteristics of a fluid flow as it exits (or enters) an enclosed chamber or pipe via an orifice.

A nozzle is often a pipe or tube of varying cross sectional area, and it can be used to direct or modify the flow of a fluid (liquid or gas). Nozzles are frequently used to control the rate of flow, speed, direction, mass, shape, and/or the pressure of the stream that emerges from them.

Curve

In mathematics, a curve is, generally speaking, an object similar to a line but which is not required to be straight. This entails that a line is a special case of curve, namely a curve with null curvature. Often curves in two-dimensional (plane curves) or three-dimensional (space curves) Euclidean space are of interest.

Chapter 6. Air Conditioning (Heating and Humidification)

Lead	Lead refers to which set of legs, left or right, leads or advances forward to a greater extent when a quadruped animal is cantering, galloping, or leaping. The feet on the leading side touch the ground forward of its partner. On the "left lead", the animal's left legs lead.
Differential	In calculus, a differential is traditionally an infinitesimally small change in a variable. For example, if x is a variable, then a change in the value of x is often denoted Δx (or δx when this change is considered to be small). The differential dx represents such a change, but is infinitely small.
Flow control	In data communications, Flow control is the process of managing the rate of data transmission between two nodes to prevent a fast sender from outrunning a slow receiver. It provides a mechanism for the receiver to control the transmission speed, so that the receiving node is not overwhelmed with data from transmitting node. Flow control should be distinguished from congestion control, which is used for controlling the flow of data when congestion has actually occurred .
Series	A series is the sum of the terms of a sequence. Finite sequences and series have defined first and last terms, whereas infinite sequences and series continue indefinitely. In mathematics, given an infinite sequence of numbers $\{ a_n \}$, a series is informally the result of adding all those terms together: $a_1 + a_2 + a_3 + \cdots$.
Mixing	In mathematics, mixing is an abstract concept originating from physics: the attempt to describe the irreversible thermodynamic process of mixing in the everyday world: mixing paint, mixing drinks, etc. The concept appears in ergodic theory--the study of stochastic processes and measure-preserving dynamical systems. Several different definitions for mixing exist, including strong mixing, weak mixing and topological mixing, with the last not requiring a measure to be defined.

Chapter 6. Air Conditioning (Heating and Humidification)

Content	In mathematics, a content is a real function μ defined on a field of sets $\mathcal{A}$ such that 1. $\mu(A) \in [0, \infty]$ whenever $A \in \mathcal{A}$. 2. $\mu(\varnothing) = 0$. 3. $\mu(A_1 \cup A_2) = \mu(A_1) + \mu(A_2)$ whenever $A_1, A_2 \in \mathcal{A}$ and $A_1 \cap A_2 = \varnothing$. A very important type of content is a measure, which is a σ-additive content defined on a σ-field. Every measure is a content, but not vice-versa.
Fluid	In physics, a fluid is a substance that continually deforms (flows) under an applied shear stress, no matter how small. Fluids are a subset of the phases of matter and include liquids, gases, plasmas and, to some extent, plastic solids. In common usage, "fluid" is often used as a synonym for "liquid", with no implication that gas could also be present.
Conditioning	Conditioning on the discrete level Example. A fair coin is tossed 10 times; the random variable X is the number of heads in these 10 tosses, and Y -- the number of heads in the first 3 tosses. In spite of the fact that Y emerges before X it may happen that someone knows X but not Y. Conditional probability

Given that X = 1, the conditional probability of the event Y = 0 is
P (Y = 0 X = 1) = P (Y = 0, X = 1) / P (X = 1) = 0.7. More generally,

$$\mathbb{P}(Y = 0 | X = x) = \frac{\binom{7}{x}}{\binom{10}{x}} = \frac{7!(10 - x)!}{(7 - x)!10!}$$

for x = 0, 1, 2, 3, 4, 5, 6, 7; otherwise (for x = 8, 9, 10), P (Y = 0 X = x) = 0. One may also treat the conditional probability as a random variable, -- a function of the random variable X, namely,

$$\mathbb{P}(Y = 0 | X) = \begin{cases} \binom{7}{X}/\binom{10}{X} & \text{for } X \le 7, \\ 0 & \text{for } X > 7. \end{cases}$$

The expectation of this random variable is equal to the (unconditional) probability,

$$\mathbb{E}(\mathbb{P}(Y = 0 | X)) = \sum_{x} \mathbb{P}(Y = 0 | X = x)\mathbb{P}(X = x) = \mathbb{P}(Y = 0),$$

namely,

$$\sum_{x=0}^{7} \frac{\binom{7}{x}}{\binom{10}{x}} \cdot \frac{1}{2^{10}} \binom{10}{x} = \frac{1}{8},$$

which is an instance of the law of total probability E (P (A X)) = P (A).

Thus, P (Y = 0 X = 1) may be treated as the value of the random variable P (Y = 0 X) corresponding to X = 1. *On the other hand, P (Y = 0 X = 1) is well-defined irrespective of other possible values of X.*

Conditional expectation

Given that X = 1, the conditional expectation of the random variable Y is E (Y X = 1) = 0.3. More generally,

$$\mathbb{E}(Y|X = x) = \frac{3}{10}x$$

for x = 0, .. 10. (In this example it appears to be a linear function, but in general it is nonlinear).

Dust

In special and general relativity, dust is the name conventionally given to a configuration of matter which can be interpreted as small bodies ("dust particles") which interact only gravitationally.

The number density n of dust is defined as the number of particles per unit volume in the (unique) inertial frame in which the particles are at rest.

Dust possesses a number flux four vector $\vec{N}$ which defines the fluxes across coordinate planes defined by

$$\vec{N} = n\vec{U}$$

where $\vec{U}$ is the four velocity of the particles.

Chapter 7. Air Conditioning (Cooling)

Regulator	In automatic control, a regulator is a device which has the function of maintaining a designated characteristic. It performs the activity of managing or maintaining a range of values in a machine. The measurable property of a device is managed closely by specified conditions or an advance set value; or it can be a variable according to a predetermined arrangement scheme.
Specification	In regression analysis and related fields such as econometrics, specification is the process of converting a theory into a regression model. This process consists of selecting an appropriate functional form for the model and choosing which variables to include. Model specification is one of the first steps in regression analysis.
Power	The Power of a statistical test is the probability that the test will reject a false null hypothesis (i.e. that it will not make a Type II error). As Power increases, the chances of a Type II error decrease. The probability of a Type II error is referred to as the false negative rate (β). Therefore Power is equal to $1 - \beta$.
Conditioning	Conditioning on the discrete level

Example. A fair coin is tossed 10 times; the random variable X is the number of heads in these 10 tosses, and Y -- the number of heads in the first 3 tosses. In spite of the fact that Y emerges before X it may happen that someone knows X but not Y.

Conditional probability

Given that X = 1, the conditional probability of the event Y = 0 is
P (Y = 0 X = 1) = P (Y = 0, X = 1) / P (X = 1) = 0.7. More generally,

$$\mathbb{P}(Y = 0 | X = x) = \frac{\binom{7}{x}}{\binom{10}{x}} = \frac{7!(10 - x)!}{(7 - x)!10!}$$

for x = 0, 1, 2, 3, 4, 5, 6, 7; otherwise (for x = 8, 9, 10), P (Y = 0 X = x) = 0. One may also treat the conditional probability as a random variable, -- a function of the random variable X, namely,

$$\mathbb{P}(Y=0|X) = \begin{cases} \binom{7}{X}/\binom{10}{X} & \text{for } X \leq 7, \\ 0 & \text{for } X > 7. \end{cases}$$

The expectation of this random variable is equal to the (unconditional) probability,

$$\mathbb{E}(\mathbb{P}(Y=0|X)) = \sum_{x} \mathbb{P}(Y=0|X=x)\mathbb{P}(X=x) = \mathbb{P}(Y=0),$$

namely,

$$\sum_{x=0}^{7} \frac{\binom{7}{x}}{\binom{10}{x}} \cdot \frac{1}{2^{10}} \binom{10}{x} = \frac{1}{8},$$

which is an instance of the law of total probability E (P (A X)) = P (A).

Thus, P (Y = 0 X = 1) may be treated as the value of the random variable P (Y = 0 X) corresponding to X = 1. *On the other hand, P (Y = 0 X = 1) is well-defined irrespective of other possible values of X.*

Conditional expectation

Given that X = 1, the conditional expectation of the random variable Y is E (Y X = 1) = 0.3. More generally,

$$\mathbb{E}(Y|X=x) = \frac{3}{10}x$$

for x = 0, .. 10. (In this example it appears to be a linear function, but in general it is nonlinear).

Diaphragm	In mechanics, a diaphragm is a sheet of a semi-flexible material anchored at its periphery and most often round in shape. It serves either as a barrier between two chambers, moving slightly up into one chamber or down into the other depending on differences in pressure, or as a device that vibrates when certain frequencies are applied to it.
	A diaphragm pump uses a diaphragm to pump a fluid.
Distribution	In differential geometry, a discipline within mathematics, a distribution is a subset of the tangent bundle of a manifold satisfying certain properties.
Column	A column in structural engineering is a vertical structural element that transmits, through compression, the weight of the structure above to other structural elements below. For the purpose of wind or earthquake engineering, columns may be designed to resist lateral forces. Other compression members are often termed "columns" because of the similar stress conditions.
Friction	Friction is the force resisting the relative motion of solid surfaces, fluid layers, and/or material elements sliding against each other. It may be thought of as the opposite of "slipperiness".
	There are several types of friction:
	• Dry friction resists relative lateral motion of two solid surfaces in contact.
Mechanism	Mechanism is the belief that natural wholes (principally living things) are like machines or artifacts, composed of parts lacking any intrinsic relationship to each other, and with their order imposed from without. Thus, the source of an apparent thing's activities is not the whole itself, but its parts or an external influence on the parts. Mechanism is opposed to the organic conception of nature best articulated by Aristotle and more recently elaborated as vitalism.

Chapter 7. Air Conditioning (Cooling)

Slip	In vehicle dynamics, slip is the relative motion between a tire and the road surface it is moving on. This slip can be generated either by the tire's rotational speed being greater or less than the free-rolling speed (usually described as percent slip), or by the tire's plane of rotation being at an angle to its direction of motion (referred to as slip angle).
	The slip is generally given as a percentage of the difference between the surface speed of the wheel compared to the speed between axis and road surface, as:
	$$slip = \frac{\omega r - v}{v},$$
	where ω is rotational speed of the wheel, r is wheel radius and v is vehicle speed.
Compression	In functional analysis, the compression of a linear operator T on a Hilbert space to a subspace K is the operator
	$$P_K T|_K$$
	where P_K is the orthogonal projection onto K. This is a natural way to obtain an operator on K from an operator on the whole Hilbert space. If K is an invariant subspace for T, then the compression of T to K is the restricted operator K→K sending k to Tk. General, let V be isometry on Hilbert space W, subspace of Hilbert space H (T on H).
Mechanism	Mechanism is the belief that natural wholes (principally living things) are like machines or artifacts, composed of parts lacking any intrinsic relationship to each other, and with their order imposed from without. Thus, the source of an apparent thing's activities is not the whole itself, but its parts or an external influence on the parts. Mechanism is opposed to the organic conception of nature best articulated by Aristotle and more recently elaborated as vitalism.

Chapter 7. Air Conditioning (Cooling)

Coupling	In probability theory, coupling is a proof technique that allows one to compare two unrelated variables by "forcing" them to be related in some way.

Using the standard formalism of probability, let X_1 and X_2 be two random variables defined on probability spaces (Ω_1, F_1, P_1) and (Ω_2, F_2, P_2). Then a coupling of X_1 and X_2 is a new probability space (Ω, F, P) over which there are two random variables Y_1 and Y_2 such that Y_1 has the same distribution as X_1 while Y_2 has the same distribution as X_2. |
| Inertia | Inertia is the resistance of any physical object to a change in its state of motion or rest. It is represented numerically by an object's mass. The principle of inertia is one of the fundamental principles of classical physics which are used to describe the motion of matter and how it is affected by applied forces. |
| Differential | In calculus, a differential is traditionally an infinitesimally small change in a variable. For example, if x is a variable, then a change in the value of x is often denoted Δx (or δx when this change is considered to be small). The differential dx represents such a change, but is infinitely small. |
| Friction loss | Friction loss refers to that portion of pressure lost by fluids while moving through a pipe, hose, or other limited space. In mechanical systems such as internal combustion engines, it refers to the power lost overcoming the friction between two moving surfaces.

Friction loss has several causes, including:

- Frictional losses depend on the conditions of flow and the physical properties of the system.
- Movement of fluid molecules against each other
- Movement of fluid molecules against the inside surface of a pipe or the like, particularly if the inside surface is rough, textured, or otherwise not smooth
- Bends, kinks, and other sharp turns in hose or piping |

In pipe flows the losses due to friction is of two kind first the skin-friction and the other is form-friction, the former one is due to the roughness in the inner part of the pipe where the fluid comes in the contact of the pipe material and the latter one is due to the obstructions present in the line of flow, it may be due to a bend or a control valve or anything which changes the course of motion of the flowing fluid.

Vibration

Vibration refers to mechanical oscillations about an equilibrium point. The oscillations may be periodic such as the motion of a pendulum or random such as the movement of a tire on a gravel road.

Vibration is occasionally "desirable".

Vibration isolation

Vibration-isolation is the process of isolating an object, such as a piece of equipment, from the source of vibrations.

Passive isolation

Passive vibration isolation systems consist essentially of a mass, spring and damper (dash-pot).

Negative-Stiffness Vibration Isolator

Negative-Stiffness-Mechanism (NSM) vibration isolation systems offer a unique passive approach for achieving low vibration environments and isolation against sub-Hertz vibrations.

Connector

In mathematics, a connector is a map which can be defined for a linear connection and used to define the covariant derivative on a vector bundle from the linear connection.

Chapter 7. Air Conditioning (Cooling)

Connection

In geometry, the notion of a connection makes precise the idea of transporting data along a curve or family of curves in a parallel and consistent manner. There are a variety of kinds of connections in modern geometry, depending on what sort of data one wants to transport. For instance, an affine connection, the most elementary type of connection, gives a means for transporting tangent vectors to a manifold from one point to another along a curve.

Series

A series is the sum of the terms of a sequence. Finite sequences and series have defined first and last terms, whereas infinite sequences and series continue indefinitely.

In mathematics, given an infinite sequence of numbers $\{ a_n \}$, a series is informally the result of adding all those terms together: $a_1 + a_2 + a_3 + \cdots$.

Current

In mathematics, more particularly in functional analysis, differential topology, and geometric measure theory, a k-current in the sense of Georges de Rham is a functional on the space of compactly supported differential k-forms, on a smooth manifold M. Formally currents behave like Schwartz distributions on a space of differential forms. In a geometric setting, they can represent integration over a submanifold, generalizing the Dirac delta function, or more generally even directional derivatives of delta functions (multipoles) spread out along subsets of M.

Let $\Omega_c^m \left(\mathbb{R}^n \right)$ denote the space of smooth m-forms with compact support on R^n. A current is a linear functional on $\Omega_c^m \left(\mathbb{R}^n \right)$ which is continuous in the sense of distributions.

Efficiency

In statistics, efficiency is a term used in the comparison of various statistical procedures and, in particular, it refers to a measure of the desirability of an estimator, of an experimental design or of an hypothesis testing procedure.

Chapter 7. Air Conditioning (Cooling)

The relative efficiency of two procedures is the ratio of their efficiencies, although often this term is used where the comparison is made between a given procedure and a notional "best possible" procedure. The efficiencies and the relative efficiency of two procedures theoretically depend on the sample size available for the given procedure, but it is often possible to use the asymptotic relative efficiency as the principal comparison measure.

Running

Running is a means of terrestrial locomotion allowing a human or an animal to move rapidly on foot. It is simply defined in athletics terms as a gait in which at regular points during the running cycle both feet are off the ground. This is in contrast to walking, where one foot is always in contact with the ground, the legs are kept mostly straight and the center of gravity vaults over the legs in an inverted pendulum fashion.

Matching

The matching is a statistical technique which is used to evaluate the effect of a treatment by comparing the treated and the non-treated in non experimental design (when the treatment is not randomly assigned). People use this technique with observational data (ie non experimental data). The idea is to find for any treated unit a similar non treated unit with similar observable characteristics.

Manifold

In mathematics (specifically in differential geometry and topology) a manifold is a mathematical space that on a small enough scale resembles the Euclidean space of a specific dimension, called the dimension of the manifold. Thus, a line and a circle are one-dimensional manifolds, a plane and sphere (the surface of a ball) are two-dimensional manifolds, and so on into high-dimensional space. More formally, every point of an n-dimensional manifold has a neighborhood homeomorphic to an open subset of the n-dimensional space R^n.

Manifold

In mathematics (specifically in differential geometry and topology) a manifold is a mathematical space that on a small enough scale resembles the Euclidean space of a specific dimension, called the dimension of the manifold. Thus, a line and a circle are one-dimensional manifolds, a plane and sphere (the surface of a ball) are two-dimensional manifolds, and so on into high-dimensional space. More formally, every point of an n-dimensional manifold has a neighborhood homeomorphic to an open subset of the n-dimensional space R^n.

Curve

In mathematics, a curve is, generally speaking, an object similar to a line but which is not required to be straight. This entails that a line is a special case of curve, namely a curve with null curvature. Often curves in two-dimensional (plane curves) or three-dimensional (space curves) Euclidean space are of interest.

Conditioning	Conditioning on the discrete level

Example. A fair coin is tossed 10 times; the random variable X is the number of heads in these 10 tosses, and Y -- the number of heads in the first 3 tosses. In spite of the fact that Y emerges before X it may happen that someone knows X but not Y.

Conditional probability

Given that X = 1, the conditional probability of the event Y = 0 is
P (Y = 0 X = 1) = P (Y = 0, X = 1) / P (X = 1) = 0.7. More generally,

$$\mathbb{P}(Y = 0 | X = x) = \frac{\binom{7}{x}}{\binom{10}{x}} = \frac{7!(10-x)!}{(7-x)!10!}$$

for x = 0, 1, 2, 3, 4, 5, 6, 7; otherwise (for x = 8, 9, 10), P (Y = 0 X = x) = 0. One may also treat the conditional probability as a random variable, -- a function of the random variable X, namely,

$$\mathbb{P}(Y = 0 | X) = \begin{cases} \binom{7}{X}/\binom{10}{X} & \text{for } X \leq 7, \\ 0 & \text{for } X > 7. \end{cases}$$

The expectation of this random variable is equal to the (unconditional) probability,

$$\mathbb{E}(\mathbb{P}(Y = 0 | X)) = \sum_x \mathbb{P}(Y = 0 | X = x)\mathbb{P}(X = x) = \mathbb{P}(Y = 0),$$

namely,

$$\sum_{x=0}^{7} \frac{\binom{7}{x}}{\binom{10}{x}} \cdot \frac{1}{2^{10}} \binom{10}{x} = \frac{1}{8},$$

which is an instance of the law of total probability E (P (A X)) = P (A).

Thus, P (Y = 0 X = 1) may be treated as the value of the random variable P (Y = 0 X) corresponding to X = 1. *On the other hand, P (Y = 0 X = 1) is well-defined irrespective of other possible values of X.*

Conditional expectation

Given that X = 1, the conditional expectation of the random variable Y is E (Y X = 1) = 0.3. More generally,

$$\mathbb{E}(Y|X=x) = \frac{3}{10}x$$

for x = 0, .. 10. (In this example it appears to be a linear function, but in general it is nonlinear).

Power

The Power of a statistical test is the probability that the test will reject a false null hypothesis (i.e. that it will not make a Type II error). As Power increases, the chances of a Type II error decrease. The probability of a Type II error is referred to as the false negative rate (β). Therefore Power is equal to $1 - \beta$.

Friction

Friction is the force resisting the relative motion of solid surfaces, fluid layers, and/or material elements sliding against each other. It may be thought of as the opposite of "slipperiness".

There are several types of friction:

- Dry friction resists relative lateral motion of two solid surfaces in contact.

Series

A series is the sum of the terms of a sequence. Finite sequences and series have defined first and last terms, whereas infinite sequences and series continue indefinitely.

Chapter 8. All-Weather Systems

In mathematics, given an infinite sequence of numbers { a_n }, a series is informally the result of adding all those terms together: $a_1 + a_2 + a_3 + \cdots$.

Manifold

In mathematics (specifically in differential geometry and topology) a manifold is a mathematical space that on a small enough scale resembles the Euclidean space of a specific dimension, called the dimension of the manifold. Thus, a line and a circle are one-dimensional manifolds, a plane and sphere (the surface of a ball) are two-dimensional manifolds, and so on into high-dimensional space. More formally, every point of an n-dimensional manifold has a neighborhood homeomorphic to an open subset of the n-dimensional space R^n.

Mixing

In mathematics, mixing is an abstract concept originating from physics: the attempt to describe the irreversible thermodynamic process of mixing in the everyday world: mixing paint, mixing drinks, etc.

The concept appears in ergodic theory--the study of stochastic processes and measure-preserving dynamical systems. Several different definitions for mixing exist, including strong mixing, weak mixing and topological mixing, with the last not requiring a measure to be defined.

Curve

In mathematics, a curve is, generally speaking, an object similar to a line but which is not required to be straight. This entails that a line is a special case of curve, namely a curve with null curvature. Often curves in two-dimensional (plane curves) or three-dimensional (space curves) Euclidean space are of interest.

Balance

In biomechanics, balance is an ability to maintain the center of gravity of a body within the base of support with minimal postural sway. When exercising the ability to balance, one is said to be balancing.

Balancing requires concurrent processing of inputs from multiple senses, including equilibrioception (from the vestibular system), vision, and perception of pressure and proprioception (from the somatosensory system), while the motor system simultaneously controls muscle actions.

Chapter 8. All-Weather Systems

Connection	In geometry, the notion of a connection makes precise the idea of transporting data along a curve or family of curves in a parallel and consistent manner. There are a variety of kinds of connections in modern geometry, depending on what sort of data one wants to transport. For instance, an affine connection, the most elementary type of connection, gives a means for transporting tangent vectors to a manifold from one point to another along a curve.
Running	Running is a means of terrestrial locomotion allowing a human or an animal to move rapidly on foot. It is simply defined in athletics terms as a gait in which at regular points during the running cycle both feet are off the ground. This is in contrast to walking, where one foot is always in contact with the ground, the legs are kept mostly straight and the center of gravity vaults over the legs in an inverted pendulum fashion.
Lead	Lead refers to which set of legs, left or right, leads or advances forward to a greater extent when a quadruped animal is cantering, galloping, or leaping. The feet on the leading side touch the ground forward of its partner. On the "left lead", the animal's left legs lead.
Flow	In mathematics, a flow or superfunction generalizes n-fold iteration of functions so that the iteration count n becomes a continuous parameter. It is used to formalize in mathematical terms the general idea of "a variable that depends on time" that occurs very frequently in engineering, physics and the study of ordinary differential equations. Informally, if x(t) is some coordinate of some system that behaves continuously as a function of t, then x(t) is a flow.
Fluid	In physics, a fluid is a substance that continually deforms (flows) under an applied shear stress, no matter how small. Fluids are a subset of the phases of matter and include liquids, gases, plasmas and, to some extent, plastic solids. In common usage, "fluid" is often used as a synonym for "liquid", with no implication that gas could also be present.
Fluid	In physics, a fluid is a substance that continually deforms (flows) under an applied shear stress, no matter how small. Fluids are a subset of the phases of matter and include liquids, gases, plasmas and, to some extent, plastic solids.

In common usage, "fluid" is often used as a synonym for "liquid", with no implication that gas could also be present.

Solenoid

In mathematics, a solenoid is a compact connected topological space (i.e. a continuum) that may be obtained as the inverse limit of an inverse system of topological groups and continuous homomorphisms

$$(S_i, f_i), \quad f_i: S_{i+1} \to S_i, \quad i \geq 0,$$

where each S_i is a circle and f_i is the map that uniformly wraps the circle S_{i+1} n_i times ($n_i \geq 2$) around the circle S_i. This construction can be carried out geometrically in the three-dimensional Euclidean space R^3. A solenoid is a one-dimensional homogeneous indecomposable continuum that has the structure of a compact topological group.

Connection

In geometry, the notion of a connection makes precise the idea of transporting data along a curve or family of curves in a parallel and consistent manner. There are a variety of kinds of connections in modern geometry, depending on what sort of data one wants to transport. For instance, an affine connection, the most elementary type of connection, gives a means for transporting tangent vectors to a manifold from one point to another along a curve.

Chapter 9. Domestic Appliances

Series	A series is the sum of the terms of a sequence. Finite sequences and series have defined first and last terms, whereas infinite sequences and series continue indefinitely. In mathematics, given an infinite sequence of numbers { a_n }, a series is informally the result of adding all those terms together: $a_1 + a_2 + a_3 + \cdots$.
Connection	In geometry, the notion of a connection makes precise the idea of transporting data along a curve or family of curves in a parallel and consistent manner. There are a variety of kinds of connections in modern geometry, depending on what sort of data one wants to transport. For instance, an affine connection, the most elementary type of connection, gives a means for transporting tangent vectors to a manifold from one point to another along a curve.
Curve	In mathematics, a curve is, generally speaking, an object similar to a line but which is not required to be straight. This entails that a line is a special case of curve, namely a curve with null curvature. Often curves in two-dimensional (plane curves) or three-dimensional (space curves) Euclidean space are of interest.
Conditioning	Conditioning on the discrete level Example. A fair coin is tossed 10 times; the random variable X is the number of heads in these 10 tosses, and Y -- the number of heads in the first 3 tosses. In spite of the fact that Y emerges before X it may happen that someone knows X but not Y. Conditional probability Given that X = 1, the conditional probability of the event Y = 0 is P (Y = 0 X = 1) = P (Y = 0, X = 1) / P (X = 1) = 0.7. More generally, $$\mathbb{P}(Y = 0 \mid X = x) = \frac{\binom{7}{x}}{\binom{10}{x}} = \frac{7!(10-x)!}{(7-x)!10!}$$

for x = 0, 1, 2, 3, 4, 5, 6, 7; otherwise (for x = 8, 9, 10), P (Y = 0 X = x) = 0. One may also treat the conditional probability as a random variable, -- a function of the random variable X, namely,

$$\mathbb{P}(Y = 0 | X) = \begin{cases} \binom{7}{X} / \binom{10}{X} & \text{for } X \leq 7, \\ 0 & \text{for } X > 7. \end{cases}$$

The expectation of this random variable is equal to the (unconditional) probability,

$$\mathbb{E}(\mathbb{P}(Y = 0 | X)) = \sum_x \mathbb{P}(Y = 0 | X = x) \mathbb{P}(X = x) = \mathbb{P}(Y = 0),$$

namely,

$$\sum_{x=0}^{7} \frac{\binom{7}{x}}{\binom{10}{x}} \cdot \frac{1}{2^{10}} \binom{10}{x} = \frac{1}{8},$$

which is an instance of the law of total probability E (P (A X)) = P (A).

Thus, P (Y = 0 X = 1) may be treated as the value of the random variable P (Y = 0 X) corresponding to X = 1. *On the other hand, P (Y = 0 X = 1) is well-defined irrespective of other possible values of X.*

Conditional expectation

Given that X = 1, the conditional expectation of the random variable Y is E (Y X = 1) = 0.3. More generally,

$$\mathbb{E}(Y | X = x) = \frac{3}{10} x$$

for x = 0, .. 10. (In this example it appears to be a linear function, but in general it is nonlinear).

Compression

In functional analysis, the compression of a linear operator T on a Hilbert space to a subspace K is the operator

$$P_K T|_K$$

where P_K is the orthogonal projection onto K. This is a natural way to obtain an operator on K from an operator on the whole Hilbert space. If K is an invariant subspace for T, then the compression of T to K is the restricted operator K→K sending k to Tk. General, let V be isometry on Hilbert space W, subspace of Hilbert space H (T on H).

Frequency

Frequency is the number of occurrences of a repeating event per unit time. It is also referred to as temporal frequency. The period is the duration of one cycle in a repeating event, so the period is the reciprocal of the frequency.

Connector

In mathematics, a connector is a map which can be defined for a linear connection and used to define the covariant derivative on a vector bundle from the linear connection.

Manifold

In mathematics (specifically in differential geometry and topology) a manifold is a mathematical space that on a small enough scale resembles the Euclidean space of a specific dimension, called the dimension of the manifold. Thus, a line and a circle are one-dimensional manifolds, a plane and sphere (the surface of a ball) are two-dimensional manifolds, and so on into high-dimensional space. More formally, every point of an n-dimensional manifold has a neighborhood homeomorphic to an open subset of the n-dimensional space R^n.

Section

In the mathematical field of topology, a section of a fiber bundle, π: E → B, over a topological space, B, is a continuous map, s : B → E, such that π(s(x))=x for all x in B.

A section is a certain generalization of the notion of the graph of a function. The graph of a function g : X → Y can be identified with a function taking its values in the Cartesian product E = X×Y of X and Y:

$$ s(x) = (x, g(x)) \in E, \quad s : X \to E. $$

A section is an abstract characterization of what it means to be a graph. Let π : E → X be the projection onto the first factor: π(x,y) = x.

Filtration	In mathematics, a filtration is an indexed set S_i of subobjects of a given algebraic structure S, with the index i running over some index set I that is a totally ordered set, subject to the condition that if i ≤ j in I then $S_i \subseteq S_j$. The concept dual to a filtration is called a cofiltration.
	Sometimes, as in a filtered algebra, there is instead the requirement that the S_i be subobjects with respect to certain operations (say, vector addition), but with respect to other operations (say, multiplication), they instead satisfy $S_i \cdot S_j \subset S_{i+j}$, where here the index set is the natural numbers; this is by analogy with a graded algebra.
Diaphragm	In mechanics, a diaphragm is a sheet of a semi-flexible material anchored at its periphery and most often round in shape. It serves either as a barrier between two chambers, moving slightly up into one chamber or down into the other depending on differences in pressure, or as a device that vibrates when certain frequencies are applied to it.
	A diaphragm pump uses a diaphragm to pump a fluid.
Displacement	In fluid mechanics, displacement occurs when an object is immersed in a fluid, pushing it out of the way and taking its place. The volume of the fluid displaced can then be measured, as in the illustration, and from this the volume of the immersed object can be deduced (the volume of the immersed object will be exactly equal to the volume of the displaced fluid).

Chapter 10. Chilled-Water Conditioning Systems

An object that sinks displaces an amount of fluid equal to the object's volume.

Power	The Power of a statistical test is the probability that the test will reject a false null hypothesis (i.e. that it will not make a Type II error). As Power increases, the chances of a Type II error decrease. The probability of a Type II error is referred to as the false negative rate (β). Therefore Power is equal to $1 - \beta$.
Flow	In mathematics, a flow or superfunction generalizes n-fold iteration of functions so that the iteration count n becomes a continuous parameter. It is used to formalize in mathematical terms the general idea of "a variable that depends on time" that occurs very frequently in engineering, physics and the study of ordinary differential equations. Informally, if x(t) is some coordinate of some system that behaves continuously as a function of t, then x(t) is a flow.
Current	In mathematics, more particularly in functional analysis, differential topology, and geometric measure theory, a k-current in the sense of Georges de Rham is a functional on the space of compactly supported differential k-forms, on a smooth manifold M. Formally currents behave like Schwartz distributions on a space of differential forms. In a geometric setting, they can represent integration over a submanifold, generalizing the Dirac delta function, or more generally even directional derivatives of delta functions (multipoles) spread out along subsets of M. Let $\Omega_c^m(\mathbb{R}^n)$ denote the space of smooth m-forms with compact support on R^n. A current is a linear functional on $\Omega_c^m(\mathbb{R}^n)$ which is continuous in the sense of distributions.
Column	A column in structural engineering is a vertical structural element that transmits, through compression, the weight of the structure above to other structural elements below. For the purpose of wind or earthquake engineering, columns may be designed to resist lateral forces. Other compression members are often termed "columns" because of the similar stress conditions.